Epic Beaver & Chipmunk Adult Coloring Book

By Susan Potterfields

ISBN: 10: 1535075996
ISBN-13: 978-1535075992

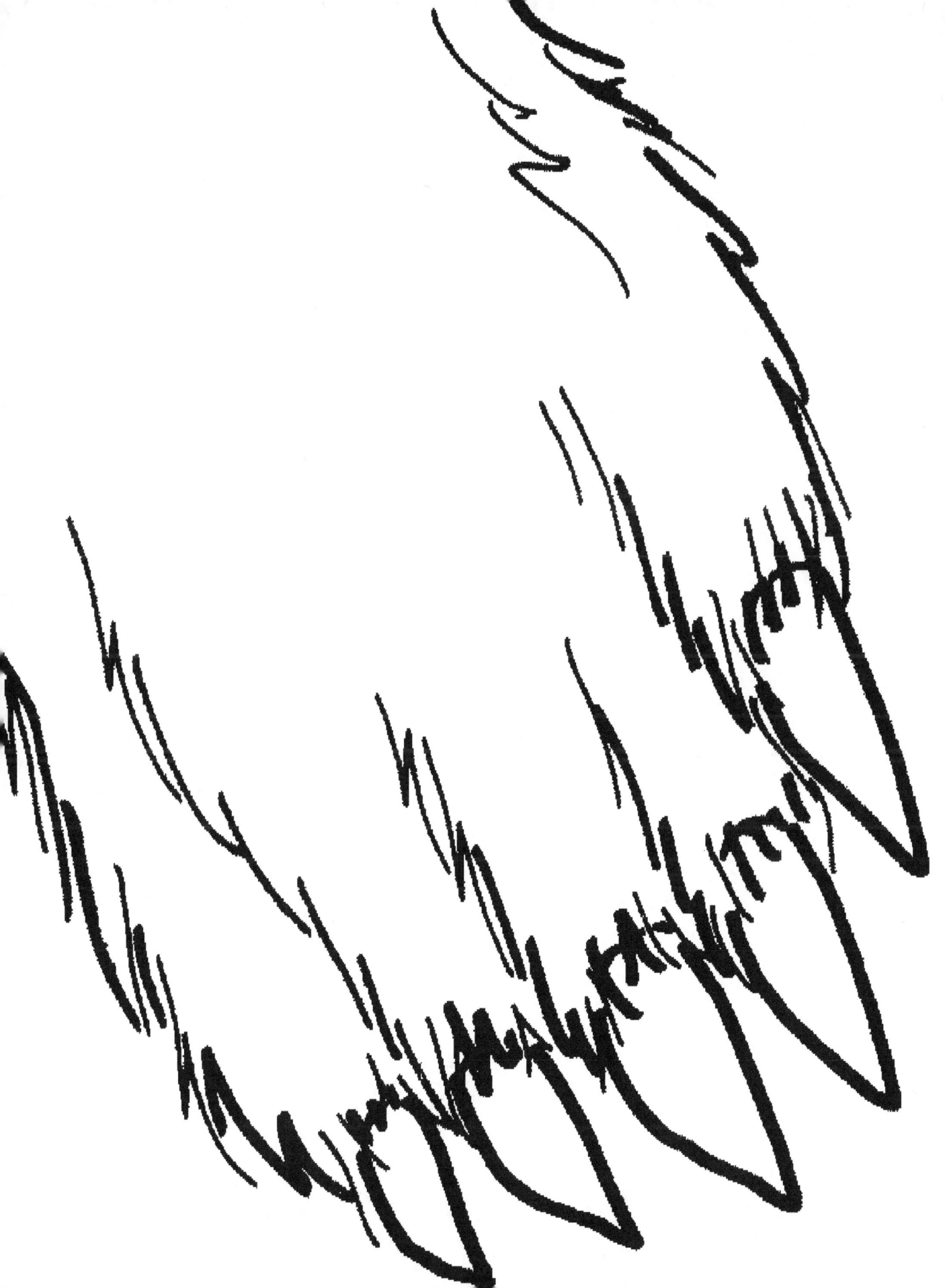

Other Coloring Books By Susan Potterfields

Epic Cat Adult Coloring Book
Epic Dog Adult Coloring Book
Epic Cow Adult Coloring Book
Epic Chicken Adult Coloring Book
Epic Dolphin Adult Coloring Book
Epic Crab Adult Coloring Book
Epic Bear Adult Coloring Book
Epic Turkey Adult Coloring Book

And Many More